# MASTER THE ART OF CONNECTING

*30 Tips to Authentic Conversation*

Master the Art of Connecting – 30 Tips to Authentic Conversation © 2019 by Shanna Kabatznick

Published by Arabelle Publishing, LLC
PO Box 2841
Chesterfield, VA 23832
www.arabellepublishing.com

Printed in the United States of America

All rights reserved. No part of this book may be reproduced or transmitted in any form or by any means without written permission from the publisher. The only exception is a brief quotation in printed reviews.

Library of Congress Control Number: 2019951570
ISBN: 9-780997-912661
Subjects: Business & Economics / Women in Business

Cover Design: Julie Basinski
Cover Photo © Alamy
Interior Design: Lance Buckley

# MASTER
## THE ART OF
# CONNECTING

### 30 Tips to
### Authentic Conversation

## SHANNA KABATZNICK

Foreword by Mary Foley
Business Coach for Women Entrepreneurs

Arabelle Publishing, LLC
Chesterfield, VA

I dedicate this book to my family.

Dad, I miss you and often think about you and all the lessons you've taught me. I will never forget one vacation that changed my life forever! Before I realized what a positive impact your decision to send me to Mississippi State University would have on my life, I was mad at you. I couldn't understand why you did it. I now see it was your love for me that gave you the strength to send me thousands of miles away so I could experience life and all that the world offered. If you didn't see my potential and believe I could do it, you would have never made that decision. Thank you, Dad, for being a father I will always admire and love.

Mom, you listened to my frustrations; you supported me and gave me a shoulder to cry on when things got tough being so far away. Even when the decisions I made were not what you would have done, you stuck by me. Thank you for teaching me how to be a good mom.

Ben and Bella, you both give me the strength and inspiration to keep going. In your unique ways, you encourage me and show me you believe in me. I know, things are sometimes challenging, but we always stick together. Ben, your ability to approach a situation and assess the pros and cons has helped me think about things more clearly. Bella, you have a fun and unique personality. Your love for art and creativity has helped me to have more fun and tap into my creative side.

I love you all.

# TABLE OF CONTENTS

Foreword ............................................................. 1
Acknowledgments ............................................... 5
The ART of Connecting ...................................... 7
Before the Event ................................................ 11
Let's Talk ........................................................... 29
During the Event .............................................. 35
Let's Talk ........................................................... 51
FAB Photo Album ............................................ 57
After the Event .................................................. 67
Let's Talk ........................................................... 81
Let's Wrap it Up! ............................................... 85
Notes ................................................................. 89
About the Author .............................................. 95

# *FOREWORD*

*E*very businessperson has experienced that awkward moment. The one where you are about to walk into a room full of people you mostly don't know, and you wonder...

Will I see anyone I know? (You secretly want to even though you are there to meet new people.) How will I start conversations? Will I meet anyone worth all this discomfort? You keep moving, trying to ignore these nagging questions and the dreaded feeling that comes with them. You try to make the best of it.

I've been there. So has Shanna Kabatznick. In my case, I was a shy little girl who became an adult who desperately did not want to feel shy and awkward anymore. Instead, I wanted to feel bold, courageous, and, "my" personal rallying cry, bodacious! Through the crisis of a bad marriage, hitting the corporate glass ceiling, and reinventing myself, I got there. Walking into a room full of strangers became an exciting way to meet and connect with the women I wanted to inspire to tap into their own bodaciousness.

Shanna got there, too. Her first room of scary strangers happened when she was suddenly dropped off as a freshman at Mississippi State University after growing up in Equador She didn't speak English well, let alone the Southern version. She didn't understand the nuances of American culture. She was in shock and afraid. It was from this uber awkward moment that Shanna began her own journey to overcoming her fears and becoming what she calls FAB – fearless, authentic, and bold.

Shanna's turning point happened when she discovered how to do something that we all want to do. Learn to connect. As a person, a human, trying to make the most of our careers, businesses, and lives the best way we know how.

It's no surprise that Shanna and I met because she walked into yet another room of strangers. This time intending to connect with me, the featured speaker and facilitator for a panel of female CEOs. That began a long relationship of deeper connecting, conversations, and coaching as she built her FABWOMEN community from a small monthly meeting to a thriving membership with ongoing events in-person and online, expanding nationally and internationally.

I have watched firsthand Shanna use her powerful connection skills and savvy to create significant success. This is Shanna's brilliance, forged as a college freshman, honed over years of experience in sales and leadership, and now in the palm of your hand.

In *Master the Art of Connecting-30 Tips to Authentic Conversation,* you will learn her most powerful tips to truly connect with others for your own success in business, career, and life. Don't be fooled by their profound simplicity. Ponder each one, try them, and enjoy the reward of turning strangers into friends and colleagues you simply haven't met yet.

To your success,

Mary Foley
Revving Up Women Entrepreneurs
maryfoley.com

# *ACKNOWLEDGMENTS*

First, I want to thank the power team behind this book. Nakita Rowell-Stevens for being patient with me, for meeting with me and helping me believe that I could do this, and for organizing my thoughts so that I could share them. The other part of the power team, Diana LéGere, my friend and publisher. Diana for motivating me to write the book, for not only being the publisher but for putting your heart and soul in this project. For getting excited about all the details and helping me see the big picture.

I also want to thank all my FABWOMEN members, that have shown me the value over and over of how important our friendship is and how important this community is to them. For encouraging me to do what scared me and for having my back.

## THE ART OF CONNECTING

Have you ever attended a networking event, and thought 'now what'? What do you say? Who do you talk to?

I am writing this book because I've discovered a huge need to connect authentically versus networking as a transaction. In this guide, you will learn doable steps to help you build lasting relationships. My inspiration started with my first awkward networking experience.

I walked into a room full of strangers. Before I could assess the situation, a random person approached me. In 60 seconds, he rattled off his spiel—who he was, what he did, gave me a card, and asked for mine so he can call me, and we can meet. It happened so fast; my head was spinning from this experience. I am sure he said more, but I lost interest within the first ten seconds and thought to myself, *who is this guy? Boy, is he pushy!*

Has this ever happened to you? You're probably wondering what I did next. I did what anyone would have done. I politely excused myself and walked toward the refreshments to regroup. I came here to meet people, but I was already exhausted. My next encounter changed everything. I connected with someone over a pair of shoes. While I was getting my food, I noticed someone wearing my same pair of shoes. I mentioned it to her, and we connected and engaged in a real conversation. What started as a conversation about the shoes became a coffee meeting and led to business and friendship. It was that simple!

What changed in these two interactions? My first encounter was with someone that was there for HIM and his gain. It was transaction-driven. It was a one-sided conversation where he did all the talking and gave me all the reasons I needed HIM. There was no room for engagement or discussion. He never asked me anything about myself.

In the second scenario, did you notice we did not even talk about our businesses until later? We connected on something we both had in common. We engaged in a conversation and listened to each other, which led to a smooth transition to talk about business. Two very different ways. I learned networking was about a transaction, and connecting is about a relationship that starts with an authentic conversation.

Are you ready to connect? Do you want to develop relationships that matter and grow your business strongly and efficiently? Then, this guide is for you!

This guide is divided into three sections: before, during, and after the event. Carry it with you as a pocket assistant to navigate through the connecting process. Let's get started!

# BEFORE THE EVENT

# 1

Before going to a networking event, research to learn about the speaker, and what type of event it is. Create a strategy for the desired outcome that would make the event time well spent.

# 2

Business cards seem obvious but don't forget them. Create something that stands out and is easy to read. As an etiquette practice, ask for someone's card first and then offer yours. There are also many apps that allow you to take a picture of a business card and save the information in your phone.

# 3

Dress Appropriately. Depending on the event the dress code may be different. Most events are business casual, but some may have specific requirements. Remember you want to create a positive first impression.

Take a small notebook with you. There will always be golden nuggets that you'll want to record. You can even take this one, we have incorporated a notes section.

# 5

If you are new to networking, go where you have something in common with the audience. Look up meetups or associations that share your vision. A simple example is a group that shares the interests or hobbies that you do.

Practice your positioning statement. You have only 7 seconds to make that first impression. Your positioning statement should answer the question who, what, and why.

# 7

If you are an introvert or new to networking, take a friend with you so you can support each other. This does not mean you go to the event and just talk to each other. Remember, you are there to connect with others.

# 8

Take time to formulate a great opening question. Rather than asking "what you do?" ask, "what do you love about what you do "or "what motivates you to do your job"? Look for phrases that show you care.

Choose your networking organizations strategically. Attend places with your ideal client or center of influence. Set your own expectations and ideas before arriving.

# 10

If available, look at the list of confirmed guests before the event. If there is someone there that you'd like to meet, do your homework and learn about them ahead of time. The more prepared you are, the better the interaction.

# 11

If new to networking, find places where you can practice your positioning statement, then work your way to larger meetings where you can refine it and finally, conferences where you can maximize it.

# 12

Think outside the box when going to events. Go to meetings where other people in your industry are less likely to be. Connections can happen anywhere.

## MASTER THE ART OF CONNECTING

## 30 TIPS TO AUTHENTIC CONVERSATION

## MASTER THE ART OF CONNECTING

## 30 TIPS TO AUTHENTIC CONVERSATION

## LET'S TALK

Perhaps, the hardest part of doing anything for the first time is taking that first step. Networking is no different, but once you get your feet wet, it's somewhat addictive. Most women wonder what they feared. Networking has a way of bringing out the bold and fearless authenticity of women.

"I wish I had started networking sooner," says publisher, Kim Eley of KWE Publishing. "While I did start doing some networking before I even launched my business as a side hustle, I underestimated the impact face-to-face networking would have on my biz. I receive the majority of my clients through people I've met through networking events or friends of friends."

The best thing to do to get started is research. Failing to plan is planning to fail, so give yourself every advantage. You must first understand WHO your ideal client is, then research. Google keywords like "women entrepreneur networking groups." Look at the theme of the events, and if you are interested in that topic, then your ideal client is too." Don't fear attending events with your competitors. There's plenty of business for everyone.

Debbie Johnston says there will be products and businesses similar to yours, but building a genuine relationship with potential clients will help you to stand out. "When I was selling, I would learn everything about my people. Everyone has their story, and people appreciate those that listen and care. This type of relationship will set you apart!"

But, what if you aren't the social butterfly in your field? Some women starting in business lack confidence, and being somewhat shy can make us intimidated by networking from the get-go. But, it doesn't have to be that way.

As an introvert, Maite Dizon, Online Business Manager, found that socializing in noisy venues where she had to talk loudly to be heard was overwhelming and stressful. "I only attend events that are right for me. I do research. Where will it be held? Will my target audience be there? I prefer events in smaller venues," she says, "with fewer attendees where I am more likely to make a connection."

And then some of us that have a different approach to connecting.

Jennifer Einolf, Clarity Coach and the owner of Bold Whisper, says she has been observed (by her husband) at networking events, not networking but catching up with friends. She says it's true.

"After I started my business, I decided that networking was going to be a critical part of my marketing strategy. I set out to attend all sorts of events. Each time, I would free fall into the room, feeling like I had stepped off a ledge. Everyone seemed to be paired off into deep conversations, (leaving me) with no opportunity to be included. I would find reasons to circulate—look, there is the water fountain. Oh, I must see that piece of art hanging on that wall," she shared.

"Over time and with patience, as I've met more people and formed more friendships, I have found that I encounter this pit of my stomach, oh-no-I'm-not-going-to-be-picked-for-the-kickball-team feeling a lot less. Now, when I walk into a room," Jennifer said, "I see friends and potential friends. Most of the time, someone I want to meet is already talking to someone I know. And once I'm in the conversation, I can invite others in as well."

Jennifer has learned that using the "art of connecting" allows her to enjoy time with newfound friends while deepening those relationships she's built, which has become a great strategy for her.

Once you decide on the strategy and the venue that's right for you, be ready to shine. There's no going back, you're GOING to a networking event!

"Don't let the last minute, "I have nothing to wear," stop you. I choose my clothes ahead of time and include an item that makes me feel confident, says Cyndi Fleming-Alton, 4 Chicks with a Website. "Word of warning—however, beware of anything that can be fidgeted with like a bracelet!"

The last thing you need when you are nervous is distractions. People have a short attention span. The best thing you can do to engage the listener is to start a conversation with a real authentic question. Talking about something light and fun will lead to a follow-up question that can get deeper and build that connection. This is true for introvert and extraverted women. It's an opportunity to take notes for follow up or connecting. Take the time to remember the amazing women you meet.

"During the event, I write myself little notes about the person. 'Connect her with so and so' things like that," says Kim Eley. One of the best things about networking is the connections can lead to big possibilities for everyone.

Angela Brown, Founder of Yeshua's House, attended a FABWOMEN event feeling out of place. "These were women entrepreneurs, and I was the founder of a nonprofit that was struggling to become more business-like. To my surprise, the ladies embraced me and our mission to homeless and abused women, and I joined (FAB) that day. These ladies, now friends, have donated their formidable coaching and teaching expertise, held fundraisers for YH, and attended our events, including the opening of our second home. Shanna invited me to be with her for TV and radio interviews, and she emceed our 2018 Annual Dinner Fundraiser. Our FAB connection is more than a network."

# DURING THE EVENT

# 13

Don't be too eager to hand out business cards. Wait for someone to ask for your card. If no one asks for your card, you can start by asking for theirs. But remember, it's not about collecting cards. Engage with people and the cards will be a natural exchange.

# 14

Be an active listener, make eye contact with whom you are speaking with, nod in agreement, and acknowledge them. Take time to focus on what they are saying and ask questions to engage.

# 15

Ask easy questions when meeting someone. Find something that you have in common and develop the conversation from there. You can start by asking easy, open-ended questions. This will help you to get to know the other person.

# 16

If you are uncomfortable walking into a room full of strangers, try visiting events that have a more formal setting. I suggest an event with an agenda like a BNI meeting where there are specific steps to follow. This is also a good place if you are introvert or new to networking.

# 17

After speaking with someone, write a few words on their business cards that will trigger your mind on how to follow up with them.

# 18

When at an all-day event try using breaks to connect with other participants. Visit the sponsors and see if any of them could be a good connection for you. Go to the food table and start small conversations. Try not to use that time to look at your phone. These breaks are a great opportunity to meet and engage with others.

# 19

Depending on the event you attend, be vulnerable and share your story. People want to connect, and stories break down barriers.

# 20

Communicate the way your prospect wants to be communicated with. It is as simple as asking them the question, "what's the best way for me to reach you?" phone, email, text, etc.

# 21

Use the same in-person etiquette when doing virtual networking through platforms like Facebook and LinkedIn. It is even more important since the other party does not know you.

# 22

Keep an open mind. Even if the person you are speaking with may not be your ideal client, they might know someone who is, so do not dismiss them or what they say.

## MASTER THE ART OF CONNECTING

## 30 TIPS TO AUTHENTIC CONVERSATION

## MASTER THE ART OF CONNECTING

## 30 TIPS TO AUTHENTIC CONVERSATION

# LET'S TALK

During the event is where the rubber meets the road. We are done planning and ready to act. If we've done our homework, we know where we are headed.

Cyndy Fleming-Alton says she's an extroverted introvert, and networking for her requires planning. "I check out the other attendees online and (plan to) reach out to someone I have something in common with. Having a familiar face at the event helps with anxiety around attending for the first time. I always arrive early so that people will come and seek me out instead of arriving when there is already a crowd engaged in conversation."

And conversations can get tricky. The most important thing to remember is this is not about you as much as you would like it to be. To start an authentic conversation means to put the other person first.

Barbara H. Smith, "The Corporate Training Professional & Coach," says authentic conversations require that we stop talking and actively listen. "What a joy it is to care what another is saying. "Previously, I had to have the last word. Anticipating ends of sentences, thinking, will they ever take a breath? Since I was always planning and plotting what to say next, I wasn't listening at all. However, now that I've learned to actively listen, I observe body language, especially the eyes, they always tell the story even without words. The recipe, words plus body language equals great communications. So, for more authentic conversations and connections, it's simple, just LISTEN!"

But, sometimes listening can be a challenge if you've met someone who hasn't a clue about connecting.

Marietta Gentles Crawford, Personal Branding Strategiest, says that sometimes questions can push the wrong buttons.

"As I was talking to someone I knew, a person sat next to us clearly looking to join the conversation. We cordially exchanged "hellos," and then he immediately asked, "What can you do for me?" I was utterly taken aback by his question. He talked about himself and handed out his business card. After a few minutes of obligatory conversation, he moved on. However, I was not interested in keeping in touch because it was clear that his intention was not to genuinely connect. It's a true lesson from the wise Dale Carnegie who says, 'To be interesting, be interested.'

Kenyatta Turner, Legal Shield Business Solutions agrees. "My natural networking style is to genuinely make friends while asking questions out of sheer curiosity. As a solid networking tip, I recommend simply being curious about the people and the world around you. When you exude honesty and interest, you will receive those in return. Afterward, the fortune is always in the follow up as you reap the rewards of a new relationship if it is meant to be."

Each relationship will go through stages. There's a right and a wrong time to advance. Make sure the other person is ready to move forward when you are.

"I attended a networking meeting, and we were taking turns talking with people. Right after shaking hands and introducing myself, a lady said, "When can I book you for a skincare consultation?" WHOA! Lady, you don't even know me.

I felt strange. Asking for business right away is like proposing marriage on your first date," laughed Kim Eley, KWE Publishing

Robin W. Kaczka, Independent Consultant, Rodan+Fields, had a similar experience. She says, sometimes the connections that happen at networking events aren't always welcome. "At one networking event held at a swanky downtown restauarant at the end of the workday, the facilitator made a point about making connections beyond the business card. Little did I know that the goal of one of the attendees was to find a date. I learned this after talking about our spouses and kids. I flashed my ring and exited "stage right" informing the facilitator that he needed to remind people that the networking he's talking about is business-related, not personal."

And then, there is the "Card Collector." He collects business cards like young boys collected baseball cards in the 50s. Angela L. Edwards, CEO of Castle Thunder Consulting calls these business owners, "Business Card Ninjas."

"You've seen them at all of the networking events – that one person who has magical business cards that are burning a hole in their pocket. They are on a mission to get rid of as many cards as possible before that hole becomes a major wardrobe malfunction. They're also keen on collecting as many cards as they can, most likely to use as a patch for that hole, or maybe they have a secondary mission to wallpaper their new office. The only lasting impression they make is the zealousness in which they go about trying to spend a few seconds with everyone at the event. Their metric of success is in the number of cards distributed and acquired. This metric is all wrong for successful networking and connecting," she says.

Angela has learned what all successful connectors know, that connecting requires pre-planning and purposeful effort. At each event, you should know whom you want to meet, but also WHY want to meet them.

"The event is an opportunity to get to know these people and find out if you have mutual interests," Angela shared. "When you exchange cards, tell your new contact that you will follow up with them so that you can further discuss your common interests and help each other. Be sure to follow up promptly in the agreed-upon method. This will have you on your way to becoming a connection ninja."

# FAB PHOTO ALBUM

Unless otherwise noted,
all photos are courtesy
FABWOMEN, LLC.

*Shanna with her daughter, Bella,
who designed the FAB logo.
Photo courtesy AnnaZaharyan -
Fire Art Studios Photography*

*Shelly Shelton, Women Empowerment Speaker, Coach & Author, and Shanna at the Pursuit 2019 event held in Winchester, VA.*

**MASTER THE ART OF CONNECTING**

*Shanna Kabatznick poses with Bill Bevins and Christine Tinker at Channel 6 News.*

*Shanna is joined by Julie Hill, Sonabank P.O.W.E.R. and Andrea Farris at one of the monthly FABWOMEN events.*

**MASTER THE ART OF CONNECTING**

*(Center) Mary Foley, (left to right) with Shanna Kabatznick, Shelly Pereira, Mary Cofield, and (the late) Shirley T Burke at the first FABWOMEN "Come Find Your FAB" event.*

*Pictured below: Shanna with Chris Jones, Authentic Leader™*

*Reba Hollingsworth, Journalist at WTVR Channel 6 and Shanna Kabatznick.*

*Shanna with the late Shirley T Burke, author of "Keeping it Real" – Pictured below: Shanna during an interview on Virginia This Morning. Newscaster, Cheryl Miller*

## 30 TIPS TO AUTHENTIC CONVERSATION

*Nakita Rowell-Steven, Communications Director of FAB with Shanna Kabatznick, CEO and Founder*

*Photo courtesy Kim Brundage Photography*

# AFTER THE EVENT

# 23

Have a follow-up system that works for you. Use a CRM to keep track of your contacts and the conversations you started. Make sure to reach out to them within 48 hours after the event.

# 24

When doing an email follow up, try to use a subject line that will grab your contact's attention. Include something about the interaction you had with them to trigger their memory. It need not be business-related. Remember, it's about building the relationship, not about making a transaction.

# 25

When asking for a meeting, be clear on your expectations. If you say 30 minutes for coffee, then be respectful and keep it at 30 minutes. These details will make the other party value you as a person of your word.

# 26

When meeting with someone, make sure that the meeting place is appropriate for your discussion. If you are talking about finances, for example, select a quieter and more private area as opposed to a public, noisy venue.

# 27

Keep your focus on the other individual and how you want to serve them. It is our human nature that when we give the other person will want to reciprocate and do the same.

# 28

IF you are focused on connecting via social media, make sure you are following that person and understand who they are. When they post something that resonates with you, you can make an engaging comment. This is how you build a relationship.

# 29

Don't be in a rush to close a sale. Sometimes it can take a while to make it happen but stay consistent and focused.

# 30

Focus on the small details; those matter. A handwritten note, a congratulations card, a small gift, anything that resonates with the other person and shows you care, will make you stand out.

## MASTER THE ART OF CONNECTING

## 30 TIPS TO AUTHENTIC CONVERSATION

## MASTER THE ART OF CONNECTING

## 30 TIPS TO AUTHENTIC CONVERSATION

# *LET'S TALK*

Once you've endured the networking event and hopefully made excellent connections, you must nurture these relationships to make them grow. What you do after the goodbyes and hugs could be the glue that seals the deal.

Promptness is important. You want to connect while your meeting is still fresh in mind. Kim Eley always follows up within two days of a networking event. "I connect with the person using LinkedIn. I always choose to send a message with the invitation to connect. "Hey there, it was so nice meeting you at XYZ yesterday! How cool is it we both know Jane? I'd like to keep in contact. May we start by connecting on LinkedIn?" But it doesn't stop here.

Eyvette W.J. Turner says that networking continuously makes a difference. "It works best for me by checking in with the people I've networked with from time to time. I met a couple over six years ago at a networking event. I had the pleasure of being one of their sponsors for their event, and I walked away with over ten solid connections. As an entrepreneur, building a strong network and perseverance is key!

One business owner shared that she keeps a monthly "tickler" file to track the special days of people she meets. "I love to surprise my contacts with pertinent newspaper clippings, cards, and other surprises throughout the year that show them I appreciate them and am thinking about them.

Darla Hancock, the owner of the Social Market, says networking is a process. "Connections made today may not be of immediate impact. But, it's amazing when several years go by, life and business have changed and so do positions, resources, needs, and influences. Keeping connected with the people you meet today may be the perfect connection tomorrow or in two years or ten," says Darla.

Whatever you do, be ready. Never underestimate the opportunities that can come your way if you are available and prepared to help someone. Remember, the key is not what they can do for you, but what can you sincerely offer to do for them.

Sometimes impromptu connections can be made in odd places, like a parking lot. I was getting out of my car, and I noticed the car next to me with a banner of a business I was interested in learning more about. I waited in my car until the driver came out of the store, then got out of my car and approached her. I introduced myself and told her I was interested in learning more about her business. She loved talking about her business, and we exchanged business cards right there. She later became one of my best clients.

It's never too early or late to be bold and authentic wherever you are!

# *LET`S WRAP IT UP!*

I hope this guide has given you a better understanding of how to build authentic connections.

Remember that networking isn't hard if you realize it is as simple as engaging with others that you find interesting. The more interested you are in them, the more they will find interest in you. Focus on building relationships then the business will follow.

We live in a world that has become increasingly disconnected, and more people are feeling isolated. Developing new relationships is a sure way to feel connected and included. When going to an event always put the other person first. Take the time to get to know someone before you engage in talking business. Always remember to follow-up; this is the part that many find hard. We walk away with all those business cards and get distracted. We mean to send those emails, yet other duties get in the way. I recommend blocking off an extra 30 to 45 minutes after an event so you can send emails and make phone calls. It is easier to do it right away than wait until later when you might take a chance on forgetting altogether.

As you navigate the networking world, remember listening is critical. Focus on the other person and their needs because that is how the connection begins. Use this guide as your personal networking assistant. It's small enough to tuck in your purse. When deciding how to prepare or what to do at an event or how to create the proper follow-up, come back here and get a refresher course.

Now it's time to act!

Research the networking groups or events that align with your business and vision.

Set a goal of what you want to accomplish when you go to an event.

Practice connecting via social media platforms like Facebook. Start with the group I created to support you further, "The Art of Connecting."

Visit fabwomen.me for your free connecting checklist.

As humans, we want to feel connected and that we matter. Whether it is in a business setting or a personal journey, building relationships will always be an essential part of our lives.

## 5 Key Critical Differences
## Networking vs Connecting

| NETWORKING | CONNECTING |
|---|---|
| **Impersonal** *No connection* *Focused on outcome* | **Authentic** *Connection Focused* *Focused on finding common interests* |
| **Talking** *I am always talking* *I control the conversation* | **Listening** *I let the other person talk* *I show interest in them* |
| **One Sided** *More time on me* *Boring — not memorable* | **Two Sided** *The conversation is about them* *Engaging* |
| **Transaction Focused** *I care about making a sale* *I work hard to close the deal* | **Relationship Focused** *I care about building a foundation* *I set up a follow up meeting* |
| **My Needs** *What's in it for me?* *Who do they know?* | **Their Needs** *What can I do for them?* *Who can I connect them with?* |

# NOTES

## MASTER THE ART OF CONNECTING

## 30 TIPS TO AUTHENTIC CONVERSATION

## MASTER THE ART OF CONNECTING

## 30 TIPS TO AUTHENTIC CONVERSATION

*Photo courtesy of Kim Brundage Photography*

# *ABOUT THE AUTHOR*

Motivational strategist, bilingual speaker, and published author Shanna K. has built her career on connections. As CEO of FABWOMEN, a fast-growing international women's organization, she's well known for her enthusiastic-yet-strategic approach. This Queen of Connections uses her enthusiasm when on stage, in corporate training, or enjoying time with friends.

With her energy and enthusiasm, it's easy to assume Shanna comes by her connecting skills naturally. But her unique journey tells a different story. **Born in Quito, Ecuador to a Jewish-American father and Spanish-Catholic mother Shanna often felt disconnected and wanting to fit in. Shanna moved to the United States to attend college at Mississippi State University, and overnight she was immersed in a new environment.**

Uncomfortable, alone, and facing a language barrier, Shanna found herself on the fast track to learning new people skills. After graduating with a BA in Management Information Systems, she applied what she had learned in the real world. And, as she did, her relationships blossomed.

Wanting to make a difference in the lives of others, Shanna entered the financial services field. But as a Latina woman in a traditionally male-dominated industry, she knew it would be an uphill battle. Undaunted, she overcame her challenges and became a top producer in her field, earning a coveted spot at the Million Dollar Round Table and qualifying for the elite Women Leaders' Symposium for four consecutive years.

Realizing her passion for inspiring, educating, and connecting in 2014, Shanna founded FABWOMEN. An organization that thrives on the values of connections, diversity, and supporting women. Since its inception, the group has grown and prospered as Shanna's "Fearless, Authentic, & Bold" message continues to spread.

Shanna has been published in *CEO Magazine*, has guest blogged for Daring Women, and her own

"Art of Connecting" story is included in *Gutsy Tales Off the Rails*, a compilation book showcasing the personal stories of influential speakers. She has been a guest on Sona Bank's P.O.W.E.R. podcast and a leadership podcast "Take the Lead," and, thanks to her unique message, Shanna has been featured on television, appearing in spots on CBS6's "Virginia This Morning" program, and ABC 8 News (WRIC).

If you're looking to connect with Shanna, you're most likely to find her on stage. Shanna spends her time shining as a speaker and strategist, delivering keynotes, workshops, and team training. Her programs focused on creating authentic connections, reducing workplace conflict, building relationship-based teams, navigating fruitful sales conversations, and embracing cross-cultural relationships.

# WE WANT TO CONNECT WITH YOU!

**To bring FABWOMEN to your community,**
**Check us out at** https://fabwomen.me

**Facebook**
https://www.facebook.com/fabwomen.rva/

**LinkedIn**
https://www.linkedin.com/in/shannakabatznick

**Email**
shanna@fabwomen.me

**To book Shanna for your next event:**
**Visit** https://shannak.com

# *IF YOU ENJOYED THIS BOOK,*
## *POST A REVIEW ON*
## *GOODREADS AND AMAZON!*

www.goodreads.com

www.amazon.com

# THANK YOU TO OUR FAB
# CONTRIBUTORS!

**Angela Brown**
Founder, Yeshua's House
http://yeshuashouse.net/

**Kim Brundage**
Owner, Kim Brundage Photography
www.kimbrundagephotography.com

**Marietta Gentles Crawford**
Owner, Mari Brands for You
marietta@maribrandsforyou.com
maribrandsforyou.com

**Maite Dizon**
Online Business Manager & Technology Strategist
www.maitedizon.com

**Jennifer Einolf**
Clarity Coach, Bold Whisper
jennifer@boldwhispher.com
boldwhisper.com

**Angela L Edwards**
CEO, Castle Thunder Consulting
804.482.1273
aedwards@castlethunder.com
www.castlethunder.com

**Kim Eley**
Owner, KWE Publishing
kwe@kwepub.com
www.kwe.com

**Cyndi Fleming-Alton**
4 Chicks with a Website
cyndi@4chickswithawebsite.com
4chickswithawebsite.com

**Darla Hancock**
The Social Market
darladhancock@gmail.com
darlahancock.com

**Debbie Johnston**
Ask a Nurse
onedebbiejjohnston@outlook.com

**Robin W. Kaczka**
Rodan & Fields
rwkaczka@gmail.com

**Barbara H. Smith**
The Corporate Training Professional & Coach

**Eyvette W J Turner**
Create Extremes
eyvette@createextremes.com

**Kenyatta Turner**
Freedom Empire Consulting LLC
kenyattaturnercares@gmail.com

**Anna Zaharyan**
Owner, Fire Art Studios Photography
www.fireart-studios.com

www.ingramcontent.com/pod-product-compliance
Lightning Source LLC
Chambersburg PA
CBHW051029030426
42336CB00015B/2781